THE MAN WHO WAS SHERLOCK HOLMES

Michael and Mollie Hardwick

SAPERE
BOOKS

THE MAN WHO WAS SHERLOCK HOLMES

Published by Sapere Books.

24 Trafalgar Road, Ilkley, LS29 8HH

United Kingdom

saperebooks.com

ISBN: 978-0-85495-187-1.

TABLE OF CONTENTS

FOREWORD

Sherlock Holmes! Ask anyone, anywhere, to tell you something about him, and the odds are that they will oblige you. His face is familiar to those who would not be able to identify a portrait of Shakespeare. Detection as an art was a mere child in his day, and has grown to manhood in our own time; yet it is of Holmes that we think first when detection and detectives are mentioned. Celebrities come and go; the headline name of yesterday is forgotten today. Sherlock Holmes, defying time and the fickleness of the public, goes on for ever, a character of fiction.

Many people find this hard to believe. Sir Arthur Conan Doyle, his creator, received many letters addressed to Sherlock Holmes, with requests to forward them. When Holmes 'retired' to keep bees in the country, several elderly ladies wrote to Conan Doyle applying for the job of Mr. Holmes's housekeeper. Earlier, when Holmes had plunged to seemingly certain death in the fearful chasm of the Reichenbach Falls, many of his readers went about for days in mourning clothes and wore black crêpe armbands. The Poet Laureate, John Masefield, told us of 'the indescribable feeling of loss one had when it was thought Holmes would be no more'.

Even today, more than three-quarters of a century after Sherlock Holmes's first appearance in print, there are those who still write to him at his famous London address — 221B Baker Street. There can surely be no other character of legend still receiving mail from his admirers. Except, of course, Santa Claus: and his worshippers, unlike Holmes's, grow up to disbelieve in him.

If a large number of people have hypnotized themselves into believing that Holmes lived — or still lives — it is a harmless enough belief, and the playing of the Holmes Game, like the Shakespeare Game, is an innocent pursuit. The only fanatics are those who have done their best to forget Conan Doyle's part in his begetting, and would ascribe it to some mystical process.

The idea of this book is to show that the brilliance of Holmes is the reflected light of his creator's many-sided character and of a life lived to the full. It has been asserted that if Music could have composed itself, the result would have been Bach. Is it too fanciful of us to suggest that if Sherlock Holmes could have written himself, the result might have been Arthur Conan Doyle?

Michael and Mollie Hardwick

1: IN THE BEGINNING

'My ancestors were country squires'

'You are yourself Sherlock Holmes!'

The writer of these words in a letter received by Arthur Conan Doyle was none other than Dr. Joseph Bell, the diagnostic wizard of Edinburgh Infirmary whose methods were reflected by Conan Doyle, his ex-pupil, in his fictional detective, who also practised a wizardry based upon elementary principles of observation and deduction.

Dr. Bell was right. Conan Doyle admitted, in his autobiography *Memories and Adventures*: 'I have often been asked whether I had myself the qualities which I depicted… Of course, I am well aware that it is one thing to grapple with a practical problem and quite another thing when you are allowed to solve it under your own conditions. I have no delusions about that. At the same time a man cannot spin a character out of his own inner consciousness and make it really life-like unless he has some other possibilities of that character within him.'

The tracing of these possibilities is a fascinating detective exercise in itself, with plenty of clues along the way.

The likeness begins even before the 'birth' of Holmes. 'My ancestors were country squires,' he tells Watson. 'My grandmother … was the sister of Vernet, the French artist. Art in the blood is liable to take the strangest forms.'

Arthur Conan Doyle was descended from an ancient line of *gentilhommes de campagne* — Irish country squires — on one side, and from Irish nobility tracing back to the Percys of Northumberland, on the other. His grandfather, John Doyle, driven to England by the ruin of his estates, had taken the pseudonym 'H.B.' and become the King of English caricaturists in the reign of George IV and the early years of Queen Victoria. He had had four sons: James, a noted genealogist and author of the Official Baronage of England and the Chronicles of England; Henry, Director of the National Gallery of Ireland and Companion of the Bath; Richard, the leading artist of *Punch*; and Charles Altamont, architect by profession and brilliant artist by talent, a master of fantasy in the Fuseli manner, able to create visions in line and colour which contrived to be at the same time beautiful, haunting and disturbing. There was art in plenty in the Doyle blood. In the blood of Charles Doyle's children — of whom Arthur was the first — there was much more besides.

Charles Doyle married Mary Foley. Her mother was a niece of General Sir Denis Pack, leader of the Scottish Brigade at Waterloo and a direct descendant of a major in Cromwell's army. He had later married the Lady Catherine Beresford, the daughter of his old companion-in-arms, the Marquis of Waterford. An ancestor of his, the Reverend Richard Pack, Rector of Kilkenny College, had married Mary Percy, heir to the Irish branch of the Percys of Northumberland, and so akin to Shakespeare's Hotspur, and, by three marriages, to the Plantagenets. Their son William wedded Catherine Scott of Nurley in County Kilkenny, a relative of Sir Walter Scott himself. For extra good measure, Mary Foley's father was descended from Admiral Foley, of the Nile and Trafalgar.

Charles Doyle invited his uncle, Michael Conan, the Paris art critic, to be godfather to the first child, a son, born in 1859. Conan suggested that his godson be called after the old Conans of Brittany, from whom he claimed direct descent. But Conan would be a little harsh as a Christian name: what about another to preface it? Michael Conan brought from France with him a newly-published book entitled *Arthur de Bretagne*. It had a fine ring, the name of Britain's great half-legendary king. It was also the name of a Conan ancestor. The parents consented, and the first son of the Deputy Director of the Office of Works in Edinburgh was christened Arthur Conan Doyle.

Conan Doyle inherited his names: Sherlock Holmes had to have his bestowed on him. His creator refused to invoke 'the elementary art which gives some inkling of character in the name, and creates Mr. Sharps or Mr. Ferrets'. But, like his predecessor Dickens, he was unable to resist the pull of the subconscious. From the depths of his mind came the name 'Sherrinford Holmes'. The 'Holmes' was for Conan Doyle's revered Oliver Wendell Holmes, the sage of New England. Sherrinford has a distinctly Irish ring, a sort of fusion of Sheridan and Wexford; and it was in County Wexford that Alexander d'Oilly, Conan Doyle's ancestor, was granted estates in 1333. The link is tenuous — but the subconscious is a shadowy thing.

'Sherrinford', however, was abandoned, and a happier choice adopted — Sherlock Holmes. Sherlock, again, is an Irish name. A branch of the Sherlocks of Sherlockstown held the neighbouring estate to the Doyles in County Wexford.

After the name, the face. Comparing the portraits of Holmes and Conan Doyle, the seeker after similarities might feel he had encountered a setback. Conan Doyle appears as big, bluff, heroically-built, moustached. Holmes is lean to the point of emaciation, hook-nosed, pale, smooth-shaven. Conan Doyle admitted that in searching for Holmes's features he had again turned his mind to Dr. Joseph Bell. But perhaps his unconscious memory had ranged back further. The famous

'H.B.' portrait in the National Portrait Gallery in London not only shows us why grandfather John Doyle could hardly venture out into the streets without being mistaken for the Duke of Wellington; it is also the most amazing likeness to — Sherlock Holmes.

It is a pleasant part of the Holmes Game to assign Sherlock a childhood and school and university careers. Only the latter is touched upon in the stories themselves, and reveals no parallel with Conan Doyle's own educational years.

Mary Doyle worked hard to rear her family and run her Edinburgh home. She was tiny, delicately pretty, and had been a wife since the age of seventeen. At thirty she still looked seventeen, for she had a durable spirit and enough mental resources to sustain a castaway for twenty years. A French scholar, she could discourse easily of the Goncourts, Flaubert and Gautier while clearing out the grate and sweeping the hearth. She would stir the family porridge with one hand and hold up the *Revue des Deux Mondes* in the other. There were few domestic tasks she could not combine with reading. It was said that during the perusal of one particularly interesting passage she inserted a spoonful of rusk and milk into her baby daughter's ear, instead of her mouth.

Her real hobby was heraldry. To a lay observer, the arms of Thomas Scott of Nurley, Mary's great-uncle, were a star and crescent. To the small boy, Arthur Conan Doyle, they were 'Or, on a bend gules an estoile between two crescents argent'.

The family pride and the joy in heraldry had made him his mother's willing pupil from his earliest years. 'Blazon me this shield!' she would say, producing a sheet of painted cardboard; and Arthur would do so. While Mary talked of far-off things and battles long ago, her son would sit, as he remembered, 'swinging my knickerbockered legs, swelling with pride until my waistcoat was as tight as a sausage skin, as I contemplated the gulf which separated me from all other little boys who swang their legs upon tables'.

The Doyle family grew to seven, all good children, helpful to one another. Arthur went to an Edinburgh day-school, where for the two years from seven to nine he bore the beatings and bullyings of a schoolmaster very like Dickens's odious Creakle. Whatever may have been the shortcomings of this school, the boy was fortunate to have a loving and wise tutor at home. Mary began to teach him French at the age of eight, told him tales from Froissart, led him to the world of books which (next to her) became his consolation. Over and over he read *Ivanhoe*, paragon among knightly romances, so un-typical of the pen of his great relative, Sir Walter Scott. The exploits of Ivanhoe, his friends and his enemies, filled the mind of the boy, and the people of the book became his spiritual companions. He realized that a great and glorious lust for fighting dwelt within him. 'I think some earlier experience of mine must have been as a stark fighter ... but though I was pugnacious I was never so to those weaker than myself.'

Many of the kings and captains of the past had been rough, ruthless men to whom pity was weakness and human life a trivial thing. Tyrants and Border reivers, killers and ravishers had been among them. High stock had inbred with high stock, pride and savagery had not been far apart. It was a chance legacy for a boy, and the boy who inherited it might have taken from his wild Irish kinsmen the lawlessness that they had left him, had he been bred unworthily. In his mother's hands Arthur Conan Doyle's heritage, that might have been spent in violence, turned towards the idealization of man's strength, and imagination gave it the power to sublimate itself in words. When the boy grew up the knights behind him were to fight again with Sir Nigel, among The White Company. The bonny fighters would put up their fists with Rodney Stone, the soldiers ride out with Gerard and Micah Clarke. A positive use had been found for a dangerous legacy.

Close as they were, a weaker mother might have softened her son; but Mary taught him to love and respect all women, not her alone. "Her thoughts and memories went back to harsher times, and she looked upon the England around her as a degenerate and effeminate land which had fallen away from the old standard of courtesy and valour." Conan Doyle is describing old Dame Ermyntrude Loring, grandmother and mentor of Sir Nigel; but the portrait equally resembles Mary Doyle.

It is in Sherlock Holmes's attitude towards women that one might be tempted to detect a characteristic quite the opposite of his creator's. Holmes is a bachelor, professing dislike and distrust of women. 'Women are never to be entirely trusted — not the best of them.' 'I assure you that the most winning woman I ever knew was hanged for poisoning three little children for their insurance-money.'

Conan Doyle was to be happy in two marriages, and in setting out to draw the forbidding image of a misogynist, a natural solitary, a crusty, curmudgeonly person, he found Nature a little too strong for him. In all Holmes's recorded dealings with women, there is not one instance of his handling them except with the utmost gentleness, courtesy and consideration. (For his wooing of the Hampstead Housemaid, in *Charles Augustus Milverton*, he may be forgiven: the happiness of many other women depended on the information he could gain from this employee of that notorious blackmailer.) Women like Holmes; they confide in him, they come to him for help, as they might to a sympathetic physician. He thinks of proud Miss de Merville, rushing upon her doom, 'as I might have thought of a daughter of my own'.

From his mother's training, Conan Doyle grew up with as strict a code of honour and admiration towards all women as that held by his namesake of Camelot. A crude or cruel action towards a woman would have been impossible for him. His son Adrian recalls that 'white blast of fury' when his father discovered that he had been discourteous to a woman servant. 'The code had been dented.'

With such inflexibility of standards, Mary Doyle might well have made a bigot of her son. But with pride and integrity she combined broad-mindedness and the capacity for development. She grew in mental stature as her children grew. As she saw Arthur off on a journey to one of his first jobs, her advice to him was: 'Wear flannel next to your skin, my dear boy, and never believe in eternal punishment.'

It was strange advice from the daughter of devout Roman Catholics and the wife of a man whose family had been dispossessed of their lands for their allegiance to the Old Religion. But Mary was one who must choose the rules by which she lived; and Arthur listened to her counsel.

2: AN AUSPICIOUS MEETING

'The faculty of deduction is certainly contagious'

In 1869 Arthur was ten. It was time to move on from his school in Edinburgh to something bigger and better. The choice was Hodder, the preparatory school for Stonyhurst, the great Jesuit public school in Lancashire. Arthur was to spend two years there before transferring to the senior school, a mile away. They were, on the whole, happy years. Thanks to his innate strength, and to Mary's training, he could hold his own with his schoolfellows at work and at play.

At Stonyhurst the life proved to be spartan. Everything was plain to the point of austerity. The body must suffer if the soul were to be saved, ruled the Jesuit Fathers; and they saved it frequently with an instrument known as a Tolley, a piece of India rubber, roughly resembling a boot-sole, which, when applied vigorously nine times in succession caused the youthful hand to blacken and swell up to twice its size. Arthur received this treatment as frequently as anyone. His nature responded to kindness and persuasion, not to threats and orders: he could be led, but never driven, and he would go out of his way to draw the torture of the Tolley upon himself to prove that his spirit was not broken. He firmly kept all mention of disciplinary brutalities out of his letters home. If the Ma'am (as he referred to his mother throughout her life) remarked on his bad writing, it was always due to an accident at games or in the gymnasium.

Sports of all kinds were his joy, particularly cricket. At fifteen he wrote home: 'When I reside at Edinburgh, I would like to enter some cricket club there. It is a jolly game, and does more to make a fellow strong and healthy than all the doctors in the world.'

No shade of Sherlock Holmes flits beside him across the cricket pitch. Holmes is an expert singlestick player, swordsman, and, like Conan Doyle, a skilled boxer. He lays no claim to proficiency in other sports, although, with a wistful glance at his creator, he refers to amateur sport as 'the best and soundest thing in England'. Conan Doyle distinguished himself as an amateur of many sports. He played first-class cricket, represented his county at football, reached the third round of the Amateur Billiards Championship, and was a member of the British motor racing team in the Prince Henry Tour in 1911. But then, Holmes is a keen and learned amateur of music, while Conan Doyle did not pretend to any knowledge of the Polyphonic Motets of Lassus or the attack and bowing of Norman Neruda. Holmes fancies himself as an art expert, able to tell an old master by the sweep of his brush. Art in Conan Doyle's blood had taken other forms.

It was not until he had been at Stonyhurst for five years that Arthur discovered an unsuspected talent which Sherlock Holmes never found. He had become an avid reader of poetry, especially Macaulay's *Lays of Ancient Rome*. Now, by way of a compulsory task, he found that he could write poetry, too. It was Art in the blood emerging.

In 1875 he passed his Matriculation examination with Honours. The question now arose, what was he to do with his life? Early in his schooldays the Ma'am had been approached with an offer to remit his school fees, provided that he were dedicated to the priesthood. She had refused. It would have been fifty pounds a year in her needy purse, but she would not dedicate her son to a Church which believed in eternal punishment.

His masters recognized an unusual talent and an unusual nature, and suggested wisely that he should spend a year at Feldkirch, a Jesuit school in Austria, to gain academic polish and to have leisure to decide what to do with his life. He spent a pleasant year at Feldkirch, learning German (thus enabling Holmes to quote Goethe with confidence), playing the bombardon in the Feldkirch band, and writing the 'Feldkirch Newspaper' and more poetry. At home these activities were regarded with approval but were not taken as serious indications of professional tendencies. The Ma'am suggested that he should study medicine. Edinburgh had one of the finest medical schools in the world. Edinburgh was his home. The idea was supported by Uncle Michael Conan when Arthur visited him on his way back from Austria.

He joined the Medical Faculty of Edinburgh University in 1876, and met Dr. Joseph Bell.

'Bell was a very remarkable man in body and mind. He was thin, wiry, dark, with a high-nosed acute face, penetrating grey eyes, angular shoulders, and a jerky way of walking. His voice was high and discordant. He was a very skilful surgeon, but his strong point was diagnosis, not only of disease, but of occupation and character. For some reason which I have never understood he singled me out from the drove of students who frequented his wards and made me his out-patient clerk, which meant that I had to array his out-patients, make simple notes of their cases, and then show them in, one by one, to the large room in which Bell sat in state surrounded by his dressers and students. Then I had ample chance of studying his methods and of noticing that he often learned more of the patient by a few quick glances than I had done by my questions. Occasionally the results were very dramatic, though there were times when he blundered. In one of his best cases, he said to a civilian patient:

"Well, my man, you've served in the army."

"Aye, sir."

"Not long discharged?"

"No, sir."

"A Highland regiment?"

"Aye, sir."

"A non-com. officer?"

"Aye, sir."

"Stationed at Barbados?"

"Aye, sir."

"You see, gentlemen," he would explain, "the man was a respectful man but did not remove his hat. They do not in the Army, but he would have learned civilian ways had he been long discharged. He has an air of authority and he is obviously Scottish. As to Barbados, his complaint is elephantiasis, which is West Indian and not British." To his audience of Watsons it all seemed very miraculous until it was explained, and then it became simple enough. It is no wonder that after the study of such a character I used and amplified his methods when in later life I tried to build up a scientific detective who solved cases on his own merits and not through the folly of the criminal. Bell took a keen interest in these detective tales and even made suggestions which were not, I am bound to say, very practical.'

To Arthur Conan Doyle, medical student, such demonstrations by his canny tutor signified nothing at the time. They were entertaining, curious, admirable; nothing more. No thought of making use of them in writings of his own occurred to him. He had, indeed, no notion of himself as a writer at all. He was lucky enough to have a short story, *The*

Mystery of Sasassa Valley, accepted by *Chambers' Journal*, but when he tried to follow it with others all were rejected.

Now, for the first time in his life, he had responsibilities. Charles Doyle had died, a broken man, genius in ashes, leaving Arthur head of a large and struggling family. He had no illusions of a brilliant medical career before him. He described himself as a sixty per cent man in examinations, and knew from attempts to obtain temporary posts assisting general practitioners during vacations that little welcome and less money awaited the newcomer to the profession. One of the more worthwhile opportunities was to go as 'surgeon' to the Arctic and back aboard the 600-ton steam whaler *Hope*, an adventure which brought him fifty pounds, and a store of physical energy and well-being upon which to draw for many years to come.

He returned to take his medical degrees in 1881, then once again left for foreign parts as surgeon in a liner bound for Africa. But after only three months he was back home, uncertain and worried about the future. Then, to decide things, came a letter from his Aunt Annette in London, inviting him to visit her and his Uncle James and discuss his prospects. An offer of help was implied. The James

Doyles were influential and might well turn the balance between struggle and success. His reply informed them that he could not discuss their offer, because he had by now turned his back upon the faith which meant everything to them.

He had been brought up a son of the Church, trained in obedience, dutiful in the observance of the rituals, loyal in word and deed. But, like his mother, he had become dissatisfied.

He was reverent in his doubts, never near the verge of atheism, which he found incomprehensible: 'I cannot conceive that any man can continue to survey Nature and to deny that there are laws at work which display intelligence and power. The very existence of a world carries with it the proof of a world-maker, as the table guarantees the pre-existence of the carpenter.'

It is not necessary to listen very hard in order to hear an echo from another voice, the voice of Sherlock Holmes: 'There is nothing in which deduction is so necessary as in religion. It can be built up as an exact science by the reasoner. Our highest assurance of the goodness of Providence seems to me to rest in the flowers. All other things, our powers, our desires, our food, are really necessary for our existence in the first instance. But this rose is an extra. Its smell and its colour are an embellishment of life, not a condition of it. It is only goodness which gives extras, and so I say again that we have much to hope from the flowers.'

3: THE BIRTH OF AN IMMORTAL

'I know well that I have it in me to make my name famous'

Far from frowning upon this doubting youth, Providence smiled, and arranged for Arthur Conan Doyle to receive a telegram from Plymouth, signed by a former fellow student named Budd. Dr. Budd was a remarkable person. He was highly gifted with physical and mental powers, but had a pathological element in his make-up which led him into strange escapades and wild behaviour, whether making his patients swear to drink no more tea, with their hands on a volume of Medical Jurisprudence which he pretended was the Bible, or promenading through the principal streets of the city, displaying his takings for the day in a canvas bag, to the jealous rage of his professional rivals. His telegram ran thus:

'STARTED HERE LAST JUNE. COLOSSAL SUCCESS. COME DOWN BY NEXT TRAIN IF POSSIBLE. PLENTY OF ROOM FOR YOU. SPLENDID OPENING.'

The chance seemed too good to ignore. Arthur packed his bag and left for Plymouth.

The partnership was not a success. Half genius and half quack, Budd crammed his waiting-rooms and hypnotized his patients by violent behaviour, abuse and highly unorthodox prescriptions. They loved it, and him. Their humdrum lives had never been so full of incident before. Arthur was fascinated, startled and amused.

The Ma'am saw things otherwise, and said so in a series of uninhibited letters. Budd, unscrupulous in etiquette as in other matters, read them, and so did Mrs. Budd. Arthur was informed that his presence was complicating the practice. He agreed good-humouredly enough, removing with one good wrench the brass doorplate bearing his name. He determined that it should be set up again outside premises that were completely his own.

These turned out to be at 1 Bush Villas, Elm Grove, Southsea, a suburb of the city of Portsmouth. It was the first time he had entered premises not paid for by someone else. In each room he did a little step-dance by way of ceremonial. He had two pounds in the world after buying enough scraps of furniture to present a convincing 'front' in his waiting-room.

Although he sneaked out each night after dark to polish the brass plate, it attracted no patients. Before long, Conan Doyle had taught himself how to live on less than a shilling a day and was calculating how this could be reduced to sixpence. He steadfastly refused his relatives' renewed offer of help — a strong-minded decision for a young man to make, on a mere point of honour, at the outset of his career.

Things were difficult, but he was cheered by the company of his small brother Innes, aged ten, sent by the Ma'am to serve as pageboy, general factotum and comrade. This cheerful boy kept the Ma'am informed of life at Southsea in a series of lively letters. She heard how 'We have made three bob this week. We have vaxenated a baby and got hold of a man with consumtion…'

Innes also kept a daily log: 'This morning after breakfast Arthur went downstairs and began to write a story about a man with three eyes, while I was upstairs enventing a new water-works that will send rokets over the moon in two minutes and they will send small shot at the same distance then it was a quarter past one, so, I had to go and put on the last potatoes the only six we had in the world.'

Brother Arthur was, indeed, making use of the enforced hours of inactivity. He had begun to contribute short stories to a magazine called *London Society*. The *Cornhill* accepted one, and Dr. Conan Doyle began to notice a faint glimmer at the end of a very long passage. He could still in all honesty scribble 'I entirely agree' against the 'Most unsatisfactory' which the Inspector of Inland Revenue had written across his pitiful Income Tax return. But even the medical practice was now improving sufficiently for him to start thinking of marriage. In April 1885, Miss Louise Hawkins, sister of a young patient, accepted his proposal. The wedding was in August.

One day, the newly-married doctor began to scribble down names, fragments of description: 'Ormond Sacker — from Afghanistan. Lived at 221B Upper Baker Street ... Sherrinford Holmes — The Laws of Evidence. Reserved, sleepy-eyed young man — philosopher — collector of rare violins. An Amati ... chemical laboratory ... "I have four hundred a year — I am a consulting detective..."'

Searching for a theme to write about, Conan Doyle had recalled his youthful admiration for two fictional detectives — Poe's Dupin and Gaboriau's Lecoq. He remembered them not without criticism, however. As he was to say, through Holmes: 'In my opinion, Dupin was a very inferior fellow ... he had some analytical genius, no doubt; but he was by no means such a phenomenon as Poe appeared to imagine.' And 'Lecoq was a miserable bungler — he had only one thing to recommend him, and that was his energy.'

Clearly, he thought, there was room in modern fiction for a new detective, and a better one: a man who could do what Joseph Bell, the sharp-eyed surgeon of Edinburgh, could do. If such methods were possible to a medical man in real life, why not to a detective in fiction? But to create a detective called for a useful knowledge of the techniques of police investigation. At that time there was no published work to supply this. Conan Doyle pondered, looked within himself, and was astonished to find that he was not merely a potential detective writer, but also a natural detective.

In *Memories and Adventures* he quotes his own poem *The Inner Room*, describing the many personalities that lie hidden in one man:

'Darkling figures, stern or quaint,

Now a savage, now a saint,

Showing fitfully and faint

In the gloom.'

'Among those figures,' he adds, 'there may perhaps be an astute detective also, but I find that in real life in order to find him I have to inhibit all the others and get into a mood when there is no one in the room but he. Then I get results and have several times solved problems by Holmes's methods after the police have been baffled.' Later in his life we see this process at work. Adrian Conan Doyle remembers in his youth those 'sudden, silent periods when, following upon some agitated stranger or missive, my father would disappear into his study for two or three days on end. It was not a question of affectation but complete mental absorption that checked and counter-checked, pondered, dissected and sought the clue to some mystery that had been hurried to him as the last court of appeal.'

Conan Doyle had all the right qualifications for the 'astute detective'. 'His mind was a great store-house of assimilated knowledge in a series of time-proof compartments', says his son. In other words — the words of Holmes to Watson: 'The skilled workman is very careful indeed as to what he takes into his brain-attic. He will have nothing but the tools which may help him in doing his work, but of these he has a large assortment, and all in the most perfect order.' Conan Doyle had the good doctor's essential encyclopaedic knowledge and the faculty of deducing the disease from the symptoms; he had, too, those qualities which were to make him the historical novelist he later became — an eye and memory for detail, the faculty for relating facts to causes, the ability to reconstruct the past from the present: all highly desirable features in the detective.

Holmes's interest in his life's work arose while at university, and his fellowstudents were his first clients. Conan Doyle's interest in criminology was sparked off at Edinburgh University by the methods of Dr. Bell. We first meet the young Holmes in a hospital, conducting an experiment: 'He is well up in anatomy, and he is a first-class chemist.' He is not, like Conan Doyle, preparing to cure mankind's sick body, but rather the crime-scarred body of Society: for 'he appears to know every detail of every horror perpetrated in the century'.

Conan Doyle was to practise medicine, but it was to be only a beginning for him. Writing often of Holmes, his own deductive gifts became more and more exercised and began to have direct and indirect influence upon real-life crime detection. The methods attributed to Holmes anticipated the first great textbook on criminology, Hans Gross's *Criminal Investigation*, which was not published until 1891, before which two Holmes novels had appeared. The internationally famous criminologist, Dr. Edmond Locard, has written: 'Conan Doyle was an absolutely astonishing scientific investigator,' and 'I hold that a police expert, or an examining magistrate, would not find it a waste of his time to read Doyle's novels...' A Scotland Yard official has testified: 'It was Sir Arthur Conan Doyle who pointed the way to the use of scientific methods in the solution of crime,' while the tribute of a noted American criminologist reads, 'The two great qualities necessary in successful sleuthing are imagination and resourcefulness added to an expert knowledge of human nature, and exactly those three qualities characterize Sir Arthur Conan Doyle.'

The influence of Conan Doyle, working sometimes through Holmes, sometimes on his own account, upon European and Asiatic criminology was widespread. The Sûreté named its crime laboratories at Lyons after him; the Egyptian Police trained upon his methods, and his books were made required reading in several other police forces; his inventiveness in the matter of plaster of Paris casts for preserving delicate clues, in the differentiation of tobacco ashes, about which Holmes wrote his celebrated monograph, and in the examination of dust from a man's clothing to establish his profession or habitual whereabouts all helped to pioneer techniques which today are in common use throughout the world. As Locard has said: 'If, in the police laboratory at Lyons, we are interested in any unusual way in this problem of dust, it is because of having absorbed ideas found in Gross and Conan Doyle.' And, as the vast Conan Doyle archives show, those criminal cases in which he interested himself personally, such as the cases of Edalji, Slater and Casement, are only a few of a great number.

So, in a long story whose title was soon changed by its author from *A Tangled Skein* to *A Study in Scarlet*, Sherlock Holmes came to birth. With him was also born that worthy, honest professional man who was henceforth to remain his foil and companion, Dr. John H. Watson.

'Ormond Sacker' was the name originally considered for him. Fortunately, Conan Doyle decided that it smacked of dandyism, and borrowed the surname of his friend Dr. James Watson, of Southsea. This young doctor was not, as is often believed, the model of his namesake. Watson, of the square jaw, thick neck, moustache, burly shoulders and indeterminate bullet-wound, was drawn in general terms from a Major Wood, another Southsea friend who later served as Conan Doyle's secretary for many years. '"Watson" was my father's Goodman Friday for forty years, and as a boy I was many a time sternly rebuked by him for disturbing "Sherlock Holmes" when engaged on the consideration of some problem,' writes Adrian Conan Doyle.

Another popular misconception about Watson exists, partly from the style of his portrayal in some acted versions of the stories, partly from the sheer inevitability of the contrast he makes with Holmes — namely, that he is thick-headed. 'Those who consider Watson to be a fool are simply admitting that they haven't read the stories attentively', wrote Conan Doyle. Holmes adds his own tribute: 'Watson, you excel yourself. I am bound to say that in all the accounts which you have been so good as to give of my own small achievements, you have habitually underrated your own abilities. It may be that you are not yourself luminous, but you are a conductor of light.'

4: ATTEMPTED MURDER

'Moriarty was not the only man who had sworn my death'

Publisher after publisher rejected the 'booklet', as Conan Doyle termed *A Study in Scarlet*. Then it was accepted for future publication by Ward, Lock & Co., whose enthusiasm was only equal to an offer of twenty-five pounds for the complete rights. The author, glad to sell it at all, accepted. It appeared in *Beeton's Christmas Annual* for 1887 and achieved no acclaim whatsoever. It is now a world classic, and a collector will pay a high price for a first edition.

While *A Study in Scarlet was* awaiting publication, its author was engaged upon something quite different. He turned to the 17th century for inspiration, read deeply, made multitudinous notes, and in three months wrote *Micah Clarke*.

'Never trust to general impressions, my boy, but concentrate yourself upon details,' Holmes remarks to Watson. 'You know my method. It is founded upon the observance of trifles.' Once more he echoed his creator. The characters and scenes of *Micah Clarke*, like those of the later historical romances, spring vividly from their pages because the people and happenings are so true to the times of Monmouth that they might really have been plucked from some inspired chronicle. Even so, the book had some weary rounds to make before it was accepted by a publisher. It appeared in 1889 and was an immediate success. Conan Doyle looked again into the past and began a story of England in the Middle Ages, which he entitled *The White Company*. Before he could complete it, Sherlock Holmes intervened. The editor of *Lippincott's* magazine asked for a new Holmes novel. In response, *The Sign of the Four* was written swiftly and published simultaneously in America and England. But within a few months Conan Doyle was able to write the last words of *The White Company*, marking its conclusion by hurling his inky pen across the room with a cry of, 'That's done it!' The book was to become the most successful historical novel written in the English language since *Ivanhoe*. Up to now it has run through innumerable editions in England alone, has been published in all the principal languages, and has never been out of print in the seventy years of its existence. The British Government made a paper grant to keep it in print even during the worst period of paper shortage in the Second World War. He had done more than create a literary masterpiece. He had realized suddenly that he was wasting too much of his life. Part-time writing would get him nowhere. He would be his own master, free, living as he wanted to live.

Sherlock Holmes was at hand to help him in his decision. In 1891, six short Holmes adventures appeared in George Newnes' new *Strand Magazine*. Since the passing of the Education Act a few years before, a public for popular literature had been growing steadily. The *Strand* had been founded to cater for its demands, and the Sherlock Holmes stories were among the first things ever read by those who now could read. For the more privileged, a detective-hero was something quite new, and proved just as irresistible as detective-heroes have been ever since. To quote John Masefield again: 'Waiting from month to month for the next adventure of Sherlock Holmes was agony.'

Conan Doyle had intended only to write six Holmes stories, before turning again to more 'serious' things; but the *Strand* clamoured for a further supply. Half-jokingly, he offered to oblige for a fee of fifty pounds apiece, and was astonished when the offer was accepted. The Holmes stories were hard work, for Conan Doyle had resolved that every tale needed as clear-cut and original a plot as would a longish book. Moreover, the problem posed had to be capable of interesting his own mind — a policy of perfection which helps to explain the compelling nature of the stories. Nearing the completion of the twelve, he observed to the Ma'am: 'I think of slaying Holmes in the last and winding him up for good and all. He takes my mind from better things.'

The Ma'am remonstrated with him, and more adventures appeared. But in *The Final Problem*, Holmes and his arch-enemy Moriarty were sent plunging over the Reichenbach Falls, to lie for all time 'in that dreadful cauldron of swirling water and seething foam'. That, at least, was the intention.

It has often been asserted that Conan Doyle hated Holmes. The truth is rather different. He resented Holmes's success and the demands of the public for more and more. To him, the stories were light entertainment, coming between him and the knights of *The White Company*, the Cavaliers and Roundheads of *Micah Clarke*, the Regency bucks and bonny fighters of *Rodney Stone*. Besides, he was too busy for Holmes. His public and private lives could hardly have been more full. Holmes must go.

It was the most remarkable killing-off in literature. A flagrant case, in fact, of *non habeas corpus*. To make a death convincing, it is necessary to produce a body. That is just what Conan Doyle did not do. He might so easily have had Holmes shot, stabbed, throttled or poisoned. The corpse might have lain in state, a Baker Street Irregular on guard at each coffin-corner, while mourning crowds shuffled by and Watson suppressed with difficulty his manly grief. But some compunction, or, more probably, instinct, restrained Conan Doyle from taking so irrevocable a step. The body was never found, therefore there need *be* no body. The whole thing was a natural mistake on Watson's part. Moriarty and Holmes *had* been clasped in a death-struggle on the edge of that dreadful abyss, but only Moriarty had gone over; and Holmes, after some useful years abroad under an incognito, was free to come back smiling in a particularly effective disguise and cause poor Watson to faint for the first time in his life. Well might Holmes say, 'It struck me what an extraordinarily lucky chance Fate had placed in my way.'

Why did Conan Doyle give Holmes his chance of life? Not, certainly, in order to keep him up his sleeve, to be produced if financial necessity should require it. He must have known that the public would demand a reprieve, but he had no intention, at the time of the Reichenbach 'tragedy', of granting one. Perhaps the answer lies in a verse of one of his poems:

'So read I this — and as I try
To write it clear again,
I feel a second finger lie
Above mine on the pen.'

Most writers have felt — to their astonishment at first — that strange sensation of a 'second finger' on the pen, when a story suddenly starts 'writing itself', when characters insist upon doing something quite different from what had been intended for them. Perhaps this was one such case. Holmes allowed himself to be pushed, but did not fall.

At any rate, despite the protests — and, indeed, abuse — of an outraged public, Holmes was out of the way for the time being. Free to press on with other things, such as *The Refugees*, set in Canada in the time of Louis XIV, and the vivid novel of the Regency prize-fighting world, *Rodney Stone*, Conan Doyle now had to occupy much of his attention with problems of a non-artistic kind. His wife had tuberculosis and had been given a few months to live. He took her to Switzerland, hoping for a reprieve for her. It was granted. As she began to improve he worked on *The Stark Munro Letters*, an autobiographical novel based on his brief encounter with Dr. Budd. He procured Norwegian skis, became proficient on them and proceeded to demonstrate to the Swiss that their snow slopes were ideally suited to a form of sport which was soon to develop into a major national asset. Across the Furha Pass, nine thousand feet up, he went skimming with the Branger brothers, to prove the possibility of crossing the mountains from Davos to Arosa, a feat only attempted once before. Landing at Arosa amid cheers, he allowed Tobias Branger to register at the hotel for him under the title of 'Sportes-mann'.

His wife's health improved sufficiently for him to bring her back to England and to accept an invitation to make a lecture tour of the United States. It was to be the beginning of a transatlantic friendship based on mutual understanding and respect. 'The race as a whole is not only the most prosperous, but the most even-tempered, tolerant and hopeful that I have known', wrote Conan Doyle as he toured America. 'The centre of gravity of the race is over here, and we have got to re-adjust ourselves.' This time he echoed Sherlock Holmes, who had greeted that cheerful American, Francis Hay Moulton, in *The Noble Bachelor*. 'It is always a joy to me to meet an American, Mr. Moulton, for I am one of those who believe that the folly of a monarch and the blundering of a Minister in far gone years will not prevent our children from being some day citizens of the same world-wide country under a flag which shall be a quartering of the Union Jack with the Stars and Stripes.'

5: INTO ACTION

'These are the sacrifices one makes for one's country, Watson'

Conan Doyle's absence in America had prevented him from witnessing the immediate triumph in London of his stage play *Waterloo*, with Henry Irving in the leading role. The Napoleonic Wars were very much occupying his mind at this time. An American audience had heard him read the first of a series of stories about a new character, Brigadier Gerard of the Grand Army; and by the time he reached England again, seven more had been completed. But now, war was to claim his attention in a different way.

'A whiff of real war' had reached his nostrils in Egypt in 1895, when he had hurried off to the Sudan as honorary correspondent to the *Westminster Gazette*, armed with a huge, ugly revolver and a drinking bottle which flavoured everything with turpentine. No sign of action had been apparent, and, assured by Kitchener that there was no point in waiting for it, he had left to play golf and cricket at his new home in Surrey. But he was unable to carry out his intention of giving himself up to recreation. He recognized the Jameson Raid as the catalyst that would provoke open warfare between England and the Boers. He wrote to *The Times*, advising the Government to call upon 'the riding, shooting men', who could serve more usefully in South African conditions than troops still practising the methods of the formalized warfare of the post.

Soon England was reading a headline: '*SHERLOCK HOLMES OFF TO THE WAR*'. On a winter morning in 1899, Conan Doyle stood in a queue of men waiting to enlist in the Middlesex Yeomanry. He was not recognized. His name was put on a waiting-list for a commission and he was sent away. But there was no need to await the outcome. His friend John Langman was sending out a hospital for front-line service. Conan Doyle volunteered to go with it and was accepted as unpaid senior physician, taking his butler for the service of all and paying his wages himself.

The Langman Hospital reached Bloemfontein on April 2, 1900, and pitched its tents on the cricket-field. Its main ward was the cricket-pavilion. Conan Doyle wrote happily to his wife that they hoped to cater adequately for 160 patients. As he wrote, the Boer guerilla leader, Christian de Wet, was capturing the water-works which supplied Bloemfontein. Before long the cricket-ground hospital was overflowing with hundreds of victims of enteric fever.

Medicines, disinfectants, equipment and linen were desperately lacking. As the fever victims and the wounded lay in agony on the ground and the fever-carrying flies swarmed everywhere, the morale of the senior medical staff broke. The senior surgeon, a gynaecologist, went home. The senior Army Medical Corps officer attached to the hospital abandoned himself to the whisky bottle.

Conan Doyle took command. He and the two junior surgeons, helped by their forty-five other staff, fought the epidemic until one quarter of their number had been stricken down. The water-works remained in enemy hands. The sick died in their thousands. The military authorities refused to allow the patients to be accommodated in houses left empty by Boers who had gone to fight with their compatriots. When Conan Doyle sought permission to cut up the corrugated-iron fence surrounding the cricket-field and make it into shelters, he was forbidden. Like the empty houses, the fence was 'private property'.

While men were being buried in hastily-dug ditches, a London journalist, visiting the scene, asked the weary, harassed senior physician which of his Sherlock Holmes stories was his own favourite. He received an impatient reply; but he did remember to describe the man who had rebuffed him as 'one of the men who make England great'.

By the time the epidemic was over and the water-works re-possessed, the censorship on reports from the fever-stricken town had been lifted, and uninformed worthies in London were raising their voices in criticism of the medical attention given to the victims. Conan Doyle wrote to the *British Medical Journal*, telling the truth about the hardship and peril willingly undergone by the great majority of the medical staff. He also wrote an article for the *Cornhill* entitled *Some Military Lessons of the War*.

'The lesson of the war, as I read it', he wrote, 'is that it is better and cheaper for the country to have fewer soldiers who shall be very highly trained than many of a mixed quality.' His proposals, which brought military die-hards near to apoplexy, included the suggestion that shooting practice was more important than parade-ground drill; that officers should not carry swords or wear distinctive dress, which made them obvious targets; that the traditional cavalry lances should be scrapped in favour of rifles; that artillery should not be drawn up in rows, to be destroyed wholesale by the first well-aimed shell; and that it were no bad thing if every man and youth in Great Britain were to learn to shoot, as the Regular Army alone would never stand a chance of repulsing an attempted invasion. He gave this last proposal practical expression by setting up, in 1901, Britain's first civilian rifle-range in his own grounds.

His concern in *Some Military Lessons of the War* was with the British Army's efficiency and the safety and wellbeing of its soldiers. In 1902, Conan Doyle found himself deeply involved in another campaign on behalf of 'Tommy Atkins'.

The Boer War had crumbled into a vicious campaign of guerilla raids and sabotage by the Boers and scorched earth policy by the British. In order to deprive the raiders of food and supplies, Kitchener's men were ordered to burn their farmhouses; women and children left behind by the marauders being first rounded up and moved to camps for their own safety. This, however, was not how the policy was represented by the Boers and their sympathizers. Allegations were set going, and were soon widely repeated in foreign newspapers, attributing to the British Tommy every manner of atrocity against these refugees, from rape to baby-killing. Boer prisoners were said to be starving to death, while pro-British Kaffirs were encouraged to loot their belongings and make free with their women, who had been imprisoned in the camps for this very purpose.

To their discredit, some British journalists took up this campaign of abuse. The Government did not choose to reply, even when several hundred clergymen in Germany, where the anti-British virulence was greatest, signed a petition deploring the alleged atrocities by British troops.

Inarticulate 'Tommy Atkins', soldiering on in South Africa, needed someone with an influential voice to raise on his behalf; someone, for preference, who knew him for what he really was because he had shared his discomforts and perils. One man with both the experience and the will to speak out was Arthur Conan Doyle. Stirred to fury by the slanderous campaign, he wrote in November 1901, to a publisher friend, Reginald Smith, of Smith, Elder & Co., proposing a book which would present the truth about South Africa. It was to be a non-profit-making venture from beginning to end. It should be bound in paper and should cost only sixpence. Every penny made by the English-language editions should go to finance translations in foreign tongues which in turn should be circulated — free, if necessary — throughout other countries.

Smith rose to the challenge, offering to print the book free of charge. The Foreign Office and the War Office agreed to co-operate. Conan Doyle retired to the solitude of his study and wrote as though his life depended on it. By the middle of January the book was on sale.

Three hundred thousand copies of *The War in South Africa: its Cause and Conduct* were sold inside six weeks. Not only did the British public buy and read it: their voluntary donations, ranging from hundreds of pounds to a few pence, poured in to help finance the foreign translations. Thousands of copies were circulated in the European countries; fifty thousand in the United States and Canada. In Norway, where storms and snow threatened to delay publication, whole passages of the book were transmitted by heliograph from mountain peak to peak.

The book was no mere propaganda document. It dealt in facts, even where these might not wholly reflect credit upon the British forces and the policies conducting them. 'There was never a war in history', wrote its author, 'in which the right was absolutely on one side, or in which no incidents of the campaign were open to criticism. I do not pretend that it was so here. But I do not think that any unprejudiced man can read the facts without acknowledging that the British Government had done its best to avoid war, and the British Army to wage it with humanity.' It was its air of candid honesty that gave *The*

War: its Cause and Conduct its influence. 'Tommy Atkins's' detractors, one by one, fell silent.

6: RETURN FROM THE DEAD

'Sit down and tell me how you came alive out of that dreadful chasm'

On August 9, 1902, the new King Edward VII made a new knight — Sir Arthur Conan Doyle. The honour was bestowed not, as is often supposed, upon the creator of Sherlock Holmes, but upon a great servant of Britain. It had been well earned; and yet the knight had struggled against accepting the accolade. 'All my work for the State would seem tainted if I took a so-called "reward",' he wrote; but the Ma'am, with her passion for the symbols of nobility, protested violently. She tried every argument in vain, until she hit on one that was irresistible: to refuse a knighthood would be to insult the Monarch. Her son gave in.

Sherlock Holmes was also offered a knighthood in 1902, and refused successfully. We are not told why: but it is permissible to imagine that, had he condescended to become Sir Sherlock, he would have felt he was sacrificing something of his independence and his cherished right to eccentricity; committing himself, in fact, when he wished to remain totally uncommitted, except to his ideals.

It was in the twin realms of ideals and ideas that Conan Doyle and Holmes had most in common. Both were men of goodwill. Holmes, within the limits of his profession, preserved the highest principles of justice tempered with mercy. 'Once or twice in my career', he says, 'I feel that I have done more real harm by my discovery of the criminal than ever he had done by his crime. I have learned caution now, and I had rather play tricks with the law of England than with my own conscience.' And again, 'If my record were closed tonight

I could still survey it with equanimity. The air of London is the sweeter for my presence. In over a thousand cases I am not aware that I have ever used my powers upon the wrong side.' This was the detective who could say of the criminal he allowed to escape because it was Christmas, 'I suppose that I am commuting a felony, but it is just possible that I am saving a soul.'

Holmes, so far as we are told, limited his good deeds to the opportunities for them that arose in the course of his work. He did not go outside that work to find wrongs that needed righting, and he wished neither responsibility nor credit. Conan Doyle, a busy writer with many public calls on him, a family man with an ailing wife and two children, not only accepted his personal responsibilities, but went out of his way to seek others. Twice he allowed himself to be put up for Parliament — it is impossible to imagine Holmes doing the same, or being a successful candidate if he had stood!

The first public stirring of hope for Holmes's return from the dead had been in 1901, after Conan Doyle's return from South Africa. Resting in Norfolk after his exertions and trying to shake off the last effects of enteric fever, he had been in the habit of playing golf with a friend named Fletcher Robinson. One day too unpleasant to go out, he had sprawled in front of a cheering fire, gazing into the flames and letting his relaxed imagination wreathe around Robinson's accounts of the legends of Dartmoor. One legend, concerning a huge, spectral hound, impressed him especially. The following month saw him on Dartmoor itself, tramping the lonely wastes and turning over in his mind the plot for a new book to be called *The Hound of the Baskervilles.*

At this stage Sherlock Holmes had no part in the plan. Once more, however, Conan Doyle felt the insistence of 'a second finger' above his own on the pen. He had the wisdom not to resist it. Holmes and Watson lived once more, and lived gloriously in what has come to be acknowledged the greatest of all their adventures. But Conan Doyle was not to be wholly dictated to by this incubus. When the story was published he insisted firmly that it was nothing more than a hitherto unchronicled episode from Holmes's pre-Reichenbach past.

But in 1903, Holmes not only re-appeared once more, but was allowed to be seen to re-appear, in fine form after his mysterious absence, to solve the case of *The Empty House* and to carry his rejoicing Watson into a further series of adventures.

The order of release was contained in a postcard bearing only the words; 'Very well. A.C.D.' It was addressed to his agent, who had passed on an offer from an American publisher who was prepared to pay five thousand dollars each for six short stories or any additional number, if Conan Doyle would bring Holmes back to life, accounting in some plausible way for his survival after the Reichenbach death-struggle. George Newnes, the Editor of the *Strand*, was prepared to reinforce this offer with one of his own. Writing to the Ma'am, who had never ceased reproaching her son for his brutal treatment of his most popular character, Conan Doyle said calmly: 'You will find that Holmes was never dead, and that he is now very much alive.' Those were significant words.

Why did he relent at last? It was not financial necessity that made him do so, or any need to re-establish himself in the reading public's eye. The old Holmes stories had never ceased to be read with increasing respect. Holmes had appeared in several stage plays, with equal success. More likely the reasons are that — never a man to shirk a challenge — Conan Doyle wished to show that Holmes could be brought back and his three-years' absence explained without difficulty; and that the reluctance remained deep down — though it had never been acknowledged as such — to banish for ever one who was, after all, a great part of himself.

'The scenes at the railway-bookstalls were worse than anything I ever saw at a bargain sale', wrote an eye-witness when Holmes returned in *The Empty House* in the *Strand* magazine of October, 1903. The author little realized that a criminal trial at Staffordshire Quarter Sessions that same month would result, three years later, in his being drawn into a real-life investigation which would reveal him as the great detective's equal at his own trade.

7: THE CASE OF THE MYOPIC PARSEE

'He would devote weeks of most intense application to the affairs of some humble client whose case presented those strange and dramatic qualities which appealed to his imagination and challenged his ingenuity'

Early one summer morning in 1903, a young miner on his way to work at the mining village of Great Wyrley, near Birmingham, came upon a blood-curdling sight. A colliery pony lay struggling feebly in a field, bleeding from a long slit in its belly.

The police did not hesitate in selecting a culprit. They went at once to the vicarage of Great Wyrley, half a mile from the scene of the crime. Their business was with the vicar's son, a solicitor in Birmingham.

They arrived to find that he had already left for his office, so contented themselves with taking possession of several articles belonging to him: a case of razors; a pair of boots, stained with damp black mud; a pair of trousers, similarly stained round the cuffs; and an old house-coat and waistcoat, bearing stains of various kinds. That afternoon a police surgeon examined the coat and waistcoat and found thirty-four horse-hairs clinging to them. Two small stains on one cuff of the coat yielded traces of animal blood.

The solicitor was arrested at his office and made the remark: 'I have been expecting it for some time.' Asked to account for his movements during the previous evening, he replied that he had arrived home at half-past six, had made some calls on foot in the district until half-past nine, and had then had his supper and gone to bed.

As the police took their prisoner in a cab to appear before a magistrates' court a crowd attacked the vehicle and tore off its door, threatening to lynch him.

Village clergy and their dependants generally enjoy the respect of their parishioners, even those not of their flock. Such was not, however, the case at Great Wyrley. Although he had been vicar there for thirty years, the Rev. Shapurji Edalji remained a Coloured Man. He was a Parsee from India who had married an Englishwoman. George Edalji, their twenty-seven-year-old solicitor son, was not a popular character. He was brilliant. He was frail, and reserved. He neither drank, smoked nor enjoyed society.

Furthermore, there was scandal attached to the family's name. Some years before, while George was still a schoolboy, several clergymen had received abusive postcards, signed with the vicar's name. Advertisements purporting to be signed by him had appeared in newspapers. Seemingly in retaliation, the vicarage lawn had been strewn with garbage and a key, found to have been stolen from Walsall Grammar School, had been unaccountably placed on the doorstep.

Worst of all, several other animals in the district had been mutilated over a period of time in the same manner as the pony. Gloating, anonymous letters about the outrages had been received by the police, followed by one threatening similar offences against the little girls of Wyrley. Amongst these letters had been several naming George Edalji as the slasher of animals. Accordingly, the police had had their eyes on the Edalji household. In the view of the Chief Constable, the letters, like the earlier ones, had been written by George Edalji himself, with the object of harassing his own family. The slashing might well be attributed to some nameless rite of the

Parsee faith. When a culprit was at last required to be brought to justice, who more obvious than he?

Edalji was tried at the Quarter Sessions on October 20, 1903. By now, Edalji's claim to have been making calls in the neighbourhood several hours before the pony was held to have been knifed had been corroborated by many people who had seen him. A veterinary surgeon had made it plain that since the pony had been bleeding when found after dawn, it could not have been slashed more than about four hours earlier.

Edalji's father, the vicar, had sworn that his son had never left the house after nine-thirty that night. The two men shared the same room, the door of which was invariably locked by the vicar when he retired. He himself was a light sleeper and had been suffering from lumbago. He would certainly have heard his son get up and unlock the door to go out.

Not to be outdone, the Prosecution insisted that George Edalji had left the bedroom between two and three o'clock in the morning, had somehow evaded six policemen supposed to be watching the house, had walked half a mile in the rain, crossed a railway line, slashed the pony in the field and then returned by a circuitous route to the vicarage, where he had re-entered the bedroom as silently as he had left it.

More precise evidence against him included the finding of the horse-hairs and the small bloodstains on his clothing, and some footprints at the scene of the crime which had appeared to the police to have been made by boots such as Edalji's. A policeman had gone so far as to take one of Edalji's boots to the place and had pressed it into the ground to make an impression, which he had then compared with the others by measuring them unscientifically with sticks and pieces of straw. The ground all round had been covered with the footprints of investigators and sightseers by this time, and no photographs or casts of those supposed to be Edalji's had been made. Still, here was the evidence, for what it was worth. It was evidently considered to be worth a good deal.

The charge was clearly proven. Edalji was pronounced guilty and sentenced to seven years' penal servitude. He was struck off the Law Society's rolls.

Thus might have ended the Case of the Myopic Parsee. However, after he had served three years of his sentence, George Edalji was suddenly released. He had not been without his protagonists while in gaol. A former Chief Justice of the Bahamas and other friends had made many efforts to have his case re-heard, but in vain. A petition signed by 10,000 people, including several hundred lawyers, had achieved nothing. A newspaper had campaigned fruitlessly on his behalf. Yet now Edalji found himself free, without explanation or offer of restitution. He was, in fact, no more than an un-pardoned discharged convict, under police surveillance.

The Court of Criminal Appeal, before which a person claiming to have been the victim of a miscarriage of justice might have his case argued afresh, did not yet exist. But there existed its unofficial counterpart in the person of Sir Arthur Conan Doyle. Like so many of the wronged folk who had climbed the stairs of 221B Baker Street in order to tell their stories to Sherlock Holmes, George Edalji had the wisdom to write to Conan Doyle, enclosing the newspaper cuttings of his case.

It was December, 1906. Conan Doyle's spirits and energies were at a singularly low ebb. His wife had died. His efforts and his love had given her many years of happy life beyond the short span originally predicted for her by the doctors. Yet, like all bereaved persons, he had been tormenting himself with doubts as to whether what he had done had been enough. For months he had been unable to work or to rouse himself to customary enthusiasms.

Major Wood, his Watson, had assumed the duty of dealing with the bulk of his correspondence, setting aside only those items which he judged might prove of exceptional interest to his employer. To Wood's credit, he so judged the letter and enclosures from George Edalji.

Conan Doyle read them. As he did so, the old enthusiasm was aroused. 'Holmes took his pipe from his lips and sat up in his chair like an old hound who hears the view-holloa.' It was exactly the same. For months Conan Doyle had done no work. For eight months more he would do none — except in the cause of George Edalji.

He began by acquiring every available scrap of documentary evidence about the case. He wrote to everyone concerned, requesting their explanation of points which had occurred to him in his reading. Before long he had learnt a great deal.

He had learnt, for instance, that the razors which the police had seized at Edalji's house had been perfectly clean, unmarked by any blood traces; that the small bloodstains on the house-coat and waistcoat could have come from the gravy of under-done meat (the garments bore many other food stains); and that the horse-hairs found by the police surgeon had not, in the contention of the Rev. Edalji, been present when the garments had first been handed over to the police. A portion of the pony's hide, cut away for use in evidence, had been wrapped in the clothing by the police. ('It is a capital mistake to theorize before one has data. Insensibly one begins to twist facts to suit theories, instead of theories to suit facts' — Holmes.)

He noted also that before the time when George Edalji had been paying his calls about the neighbourhood, a few hours before he was alleged to have committed his crime, it had rained, which accounted quite simply for the traces of black mud found on his boots and trouser cuffs. What had not been found on either had been any traces of the yellowish-red soil, or the sand and clay, which abounded in the fields surrounding that in which the pony had been maimed. There were such traces only on one boot — that which the policeman had pressed into the ground at the scene of the crime, in order to obtain an impression.

('Knowledge of Geology — Practical, but limited. Tells at a glance different soils from each other. After walks had shown me splashes upon his trousers, and told me by their colour and consistency in what part of London he had received them.' — Watson. 'There is no branch of detective science which is so important and so much neglected as the art of tracing footsteps' — Holmes.)

The seemingly impressive testimony of the handwriting expert did not impress Conan Doyle at all. The case of Adolf Beck, in which that gentleman had played so

prominent a part, was familiar to him. ('As a rule, when I have heard some slight indication of the course of events I am able to guide myself by the thousands of other similar cases which occur to my memory' — Holmes.) Beck was the man, who, innocently stepping out of his house to buy a newspaper, had been 'recognized' by a passing woman as the man who had swindled her. Brought to trial, he had been similarly identified by numerous other women. Gurrin, the handwriting expert, had identified the writing on vital cheques as having been done by Beck, in a disguised hand. It is sufficient to add that Beck had been imprisoned for his 'crimes', had served his sentence, had been imprisoned again on similar charges, and had been released, suddenly and dramatically, when unmistakable evidence had come to light that all the crimes for which he had been sent to prison on each occasion had been committed by someone else! Conan Doyle remembered the name of Gurrin, and was by no means satisfied that the anonymous letters attributed to George Edalji had been written by him.

By January, 1907, Conan Doyle had become sufficiently convinced that a gross miscarriage of justice had occurred. He had read every word that had been written or printed about the Edalji case; had questioned all those who had taken part in it. Not until every fact had been examined dispassionately from every angle, had he allowed himself to meet and question the man at the centre of it all. He wrote later: 'He had come to my hotel by appointment, but I had been delayed, and he was passing the time by reading the paper. I recognized my man by his dark face, so I stood and observed him. He held the paper close to his eyes and rather sideways, proving not only a high degree of myopia, but marked astigmatism. The idea of such a man scouring fields at night and assaulting cattle while avoiding the watchful police was ludicrous to anyone who can imagine what the world looks like to eyes with myopia of eight dioptres.'

On January 11, 1907, the *Daily Telegraph* published the first part of an 18,000 word summing-up by Conan Doyle of all he had discovered and deduced about the case. An editorial comment the following day drew the inescapable parallel: 'So, Sherlock Holmes is having one more "Last Adventure", and this time in real life!... One has often wondered, in reading the Sherlock Holmes stories, whether the skill which unfolds the process of detection from data invented by the author, would have any success if set to work upon data provided by others. Well, here, in this "special investigation" of "the case of Mr. Edalji", Sir Conan Doyle is putting himself to the test. It is a tribute to the force with which he has impressed the personality of his hero upon the reader's mind that one instinctively merges the creator in his creation, and thinks of this special investigation as the work of the great Sherlock. So far as the story goes at present, nobody who makes this identification will be disappointed.'

Point by point, Conan Doyle denounced the young man's persecution as a modern equivalent of the Dreyfus Case, with a handwriting 'expert' in the forefront and colour prejudice substituted for anti-Semitism. He castigated the police — especially the Chief Constable of Staffordshire — for prejudice, deceit and incompetence, and poured scorn upon the action of the Home Office in releasing Edalji quietly and ignominiously when it found it could no longer hold him with justification.

The outcome of the Edalji disclosures was a sensation which echoed throughout Britain. Legal authorities, politicians and men in the street joined in a clamour for an official explanation of the scandalous act of releasing Edalji but neglecting to pardon or compensate him. The Home Office, however much it would have liked to, could not remain silent. Conan Doyle was invited to a private meeting with the Home Secretary, Herbert Gladstone, the son of the great Prime Minister. He was received courteously and left content in the knowledge that an impartial committee of three would soon sit to examine the case in all its aspects.

He did not sit back to wait, however. He continued inquiries in the Great Wyrley district itself, hoping to discover the proof that would over-ride any last remaining doubt about the injustice of Edalji's conviction — the identity of the real slasher. He was not left long in doubt that he was close to the right trail. Letters addressed to himself began to arrive. 'I know from a detective of Scotland Yard that if you write to Gladstone and say you find Edalji is guilty after all they will make you a lord next year. Is it not better to be a lord than to run the risk of losing kidneys and liver. Think of all the ghoulish murders that are committed, why then should you escape?'

Such letters brought Conan Doyle no fear. He knew that if they continued the writer might let slip a clue. He did. A letter arrived containing a sneering reference to a former headmaster of Walsall Grammar School. This, together with the odd circumstance of the Grammar School key having been laid on the Edalji's doorstep during their earlier persecution, and an earlier anonymous letter actually received by the headmaster gave Conan Doyle the link he was seeking. He inquired from the school whether there had been a boy at the school during the early 1890's who had held a particular grudge against the headmaster, was known to have a vicious nature, and had subsequently gone to sea. There had. 'Peter Hudson', as Conan Doyle chose to name him, rather than publish his real name, had been expelled at the age of thirteen as beyond control. He had been known to forge letters, and one of his delights had been to rip with a knife the furnishings of railway carriages. He had subsequently been apprenticed to a butcher, and had then gone to sea, serving part of his time in cattle ships, thus adding to his experience of handling animals.

Conan Doyle's deduction of a connection with the sea was worthy of Holmes at his best. He had noted that three of the anonymous letters had contained references to the pleasures of the seagoing life; and that one of the hoaxes against the Edaljis had been a bogus advertisement in a Blackpool newspaper. Blackpool, it had not escaped him, was the pleasure resort of the sea-port of Liverpool. It was, indeed, from Liverpool that

'Peter Hudson's' first ship had sailed, from the date of which event the hoaxes had ceased abruptly, not resuming until 1903, when, as Conan Doyle discovered, 'Hudson' had retired from the sea.

As a final stroke, Conan Doyle obtained possession of a large horse-lancet which a woman friend of 'Peter Hudson's' family remembered having been shown by the young man at the very time of the cattle-slashing in 1903.

'Now the wounds in all the outrages up to August 18th were of a very peculiar character', wrote Conan Doyle (and we seem to hear the high-pitched, strident voice of Holmes, delivering one of his patient explanations to an admiring Watson). 'In every case there was a shallow incision; it had cut through skin and muscles, but had not penetrated the gut. Had an ordinary cutting-weapon been used, it must certainly in *some* instance have penetrated far enough to pierce the gut with its point or edge. Note that the blade of the horse-lancet is like this:

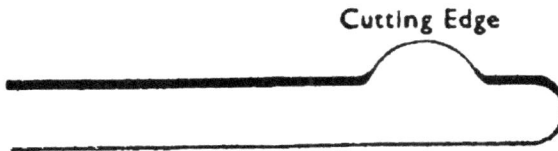

Cutting Edge

'It is very sharp. Yet it could never penetrate more than superficially. I submit this very large horse-lancet, obtained by Peter Hudson from the cattle-ship, as being the only kind of instrument which could have committed all the crimes.'

The above are only some of the salient points of a mass of evidence, all pointing towards one man. 'When you follow two separate chains of thought, Watson, you will find some point of intersection which should approximate to the truth.' Conan Doyle had followed not two, but numerous chains of thought and circumstance, and all intersected. Those which he did not choose to publish in his detailed newspaper account of the investigation he submitted privately to the Home Office.

The committee of three investigators concluded its deliberations and presented its findings to the Home Secretary. That gentleman studied the report and reached his decision. It was published in a printed document. The jury who had convicted George Edalji of horse-maiming had been at fault; *but* there remained no reason to doubt that Edalji had written the anonymous letters. He had 'to some extent brought his troubles on himself'. Therefore, he would be pardoned, but granted no compensation whatsoever.

Conan Doyle returned angrily to the Home Office. He was smugly referred to the findings of the committee and assured that nothing further could be done.

'They say that genius is an infinite capacity for taking pains. It's a very bad definition, but it does apply to detective work', remarked Holmes. Conan Doyle had taken infinite pains. He had devoted months to the case of George Edalji, at the cost of all other work. Every penny he had spent in the investigation had been his own. He was not going to give up now.

For three more months he battled on, writing articles, letters, engaging Dr. Lindsay Johnson, Europe's foremost handwriting expert to compare the specimens of 'Peter Hudson's' handwriting which he had managed to obtain against the handwriting of the anonymous letters. That expert had no hesitation in confirming his belief that the letters had been written by Hudson and his brother. The Law Society gave Edalji leave to practise his profession again. The *Daily Telegraph* raised a subscription for him. Letters were published from all manner of people, and questions were asked in Parliament. But, as Sherlock Holmes was well aware, 'It is always awkward doing business with an alias.' The authorities refused to admit that any case existed against Peter Hudson'. Conan Doyle, therefore, was powerless to name him. The Case of the Myopic Parsee could be carried no further, though the circumstances attending it resulted at last in the setting up of the long-awaited Court of Criminal Appeal.

One last gesture could be made. When Conan Doyle re-married quietly on September 18, 1907, George Edalji was among the guests at his reception.

'*Sherlock Holmes Quietly Married*', ran one newspaper's headline. Jean Leckie and Arthur Conan Doyle had first met in 1897 and had loved one another almost from that moment with a love that belonged more to the realm of romance than to everyday life. Now their constancy and scrupulous regard for his first wife were rewarded.

8: THE CASE OF THE DIAMOND CRESCENT

'I assure you, Watson, without affectation, that the status off my client is a matter off less moment to me than the interest of his case.'

Conan Doyle had not been long married when he found himself embroiled in another fight for a misjudged man. He did not seek the combat. His success in the Edalji affair had not left him with a thirst for such things. On the contrary, he took up his weapons with reluctance. Edalji had been a poor wretch. Oscar Slater was a man of the world, a gambler and adventurer whose seamy character had been his downfall; a type of man not likely to inspire Conan Doyle's instinctive sympathy.

'I am the last and highest court of appeal in detection,' said Holmes. It was as a result of Conan Doyle's success on Edalji's behalf that he was approached by Oscar Slater's lawyers when all else had failed them.

Without committing himself, he consented to read the papers of the case. It took him no time at all to recognize that the proceedings in the High Court of Justiciary in Edinburgh in May 1909 had ended in perhaps the most disgraceful miscarriage of justice ever perpetrated in Great Britain.

The Case of the Diamond Crescent, to give it a Holmesian title, had begun the year before in the Glasgow flat of a wealthy old lady, Miss Marion Gilchrist, who lived with one servant, named Helen Lambie. Lambie had slipped out one evening to buy a newspaper. Neighbours, named Adams, had heard noises in Miss Gilchrist's flat and Mr. Adams, forgetting to put on his spectacles, without which he was short-sighted, had gone to see if all was well. He had found the door locked. The old lady was well known for her fear of robbery, and her door was well equipped with spring locks, bolts and chains. While Adams was ringing the bell but getting no answer, Helen Lambie returned. Seemingly unconcerned by the neighbour's fears, she went in. Adams stayed hesitating upon the mat, and as he did so a young man walked casually out of the flat, then suddenly dashed down the stairs to the street and away.

Lambie's screams brought Adams to where the old lady's body lay. Her head and face had been smashed to pulp by a rain of blows. There were no signs of a struggle. Miss Gilchrist appeared to have been sitting reading a magazine which she had laid aside, taking off her spectacles, before being attacked. In the adjoining bedroom a gas lamp had been lighted, evidently by the murderer. Valuable jewellery, of which Miss Gilchrist had possessed a great deal, lay undisturbed in a glass dish on the dressing table. A box in which private documents had been kept had been broken open and the papers lay strewn about the floor. Nothing appeared to be missing except one diamond crescent brooch.

Neither Adams nor Lambie was able to give a clear description of the man both had seen leaving the flat. However, the police were approached by a fourteen-year-old girl, Mary Barrowman, who claimed to have been passing the house at the time. A man had come running out, and although it had been a dark, wet December evening, and her brief encounter had taken place in a poorly lit street, she was able to offer a precise description of him. Her account differed so much from that of Lambie and Adams that the police assumed that two men had been concerned in the crime, one having left the flat before the other.

Neither description produced any results when circulated; but a description of the missing brooch brought consequences which were to have far-reaching effects. A man named M'Lean called at Glasgow Central Police Station to report that a German Jew, known to him as Oscar, had pawned a diamond brooch resembling the missing one. Led by M'Lean, police hastened to Oscar's flat, only to find that he had left that very night for Liverpool, accompanied by his mistress and all their belongings.

'It is a capital mistake to theorize before you have all the evidence,' Holmes reminds us repeatedly. This was precisely the mistake made by the Glasgow police at this point. A diamond brooch had been stolen from a murdered woman's flat. Oscar had pawned a diamond brooch and had then fled. Obviously, Oscar was the man they wanted.

The assumption was justified up to a point: it opened a line of investigation which might have led to the speedy arrest of a fleeing murderer. But the brooch pawned by Oscar was recovered and declared at once by Helen Lambie to be quite different from the stolen one. Moreover, inquiries revealed that Oscar's brooch had been in continuous pawn since before the murder. It was also found that the 'fugitive' and his lady had been planning quite openly for some weeks to leave their flat and had only been waiting for new tenants, who had arrived on the very day of the murder. At Liverpool they had registered under the name of Slater, the name by which Oscar had chosen to be known in Glasgow out of consideration for those who could not pronounce his real name — Leschziner. He was, in fact, a German Jew who had lived in Britain for some years. He had run gambling clubs and perhaps worse. His whole reason for wishing to leave Scotland so abruptly, it seemed, was a desire to evade pursuit by his lawful wife and, with his faithful French-born Antoine, to get to America and make a new start. ('We have in this case one singular incident coming close to the heels of another singular incident. The police are making the mistake of concentrating their attention upon the second.' — Holmes)

It was all innocent enough, if a trifle disreputable, and the positive rebuttal of the suspicions regarding the diamond brooch should perhaps have been enough to satisfy the Glasgow police that Oscar Slater was not their man. If they wanted further confirmation, he bore no resemblance to either description circulated after the murder, being most unmistakably 'foreign' in appearance; he had been unknown to Miss Gilchrist, and could therefore not have entered her flat except by breaking into it — and there had been no break-in; and a fleeing murderer would scarcely have registered at an hotel under his own name.

Unhappily for Oscar Slater, the police could not bring themselves to admit that so smartly-solved a case had not been solved at all. They had no inkling of a substitute for Slater as suspect. Instead of taking a leaf out of any Sherlock Holmes investigation and telling themselves that, having eliminated the impossible, they must look for the truth, however improbable, in whatever remained, they proceeded to pin the case upon Slater. No doubt the intention was not as blunt as that; but, unhappily for an innocent man's life, such was the effect of what they now did. ('Don't you think it may be a little premature? I can't help thinking that your evidence is not complete.' — Holmes)

Slater and Antoine had already sailed for America, making, quite openly, a voyage which had been booked weeks before. The Glasgow police cabled to New York asking for the couple to be arrested and searched for pawn tickets. Meanwhile arrangements were made for Adams, Helen Lambie and Mary Barrowman to sail to America to identify the suspect. Their memory of the man each claimed to have seen on the night of the murder was not considered enough for this purpose: they were shown photographs of Oscar Slater to remind them!

New York police officers arrested Slater and Antoine. When the identifiers had at length arrived Slater was brought from the Tombs Prison, handcuffed to a U.S. Marshal, and led along a corridor in which the two girls were stationed. Both of them identified him at once. Slater's fate was sealed.

With a moral record such as his, Oscar Slater was already half convicted in the eyes of a large proportion of Scottish opinion of any charge which anyone might have cared to bring against him, from fratricide to stealing coins from a gas-meter. ('How deceptive appearances may be, to be sure!' — Holmes)

Prosecuting him in Edinburgh, Lord Advocate Ure did not hesitate to use every scrap of evidence, however dubious, which might in any way reflect a possibility of suspicion against Slater. Slater had been picked out at identity parades — the men chosen to line up with him had been as unlike this unmistakable foreigner as it could have been possible to get them; Slater had been identified in New York by Lambie and Barrowman, both of whom had studied photographs of him, had altered their evidence as to what they had seen on the night of the murder, and had demonstrated their probity and honour by claiming, in all seriousness, that they had never once discussed the case together while sharing a cabin on board a ship taking them to America for the express purpose of identifying the suspect!

Slater had been found to possess a small tin-tack hammer. Not one trace of blood had been discovered upon it; but this, in the Prosecution's contention, had obviously been used to batter a woman's head to pulp. A man had been seen loitering in the street near Miss Gilchrist's house on several occasions; descriptions of him had nothing in common with Slater and accounts of his dress had differed widely; but, having been shown photographs of Slater in advance, a succession of witnesses unashamedly identified him. Significantly, a woman witness whose evidence did not at all fit in with the case against Slater was never called. Nor did the Crown see fit to call the doctor who had examined Miss Gilchrist, and in whose opinion the weapon used had been not a little hammer such as Slater had possessed, but a heavy mahogany chair-leg, such as had *not* been found amongst Slater's belongings.

Such was the tenor and quality of the Lord Advocate's case against the prisoner in the dock. Its many inaccuracies, omissions and illogicalities were allowed by the judge, Lord Guthrie, to go completely unchecked. If Ure himself was conscious of any flaws in his case, he did not allow them to undermine his confidence. He made a passionate plea for a conviction.

By comparison, the case for Slater sounded tame. He was not allowed to go into the witness-box and speak for himself; it is doubtful whether his thick guttural accent would have helped to lessen the prejudice in that court room. As for the impartiality of the judge's summing-up, Lord Guthrie demonstrated his intentions in the matter right from the start: 'Up to yesterday afternoon I should have thought that there was one serious difficulty which confronted you — the difficulty of conceiving that there was in existence a human being capable of doing such a dastardly deed. Gentlemen, that difficulty, I think, was removed when we heard from the lips of one who seemingly knew the prisoner better than anyone else, that he had followed a life which descends to the very lowest

61

depths of human degradation, for by the universal judgment of mankind, the man who lives upon the proceeds of prostitution has sunk to the lowest depths, and all moral sense has been destroyed and has ceased to exist. That difficulty removed, I say without hesitation that the man in the dock is capable of having committed this dastardly outrage.'

The implication that Slater had been living on the earnings of a prostitute came from a vague piece of evidence which the judge should by rights have disallowed as hearsay, let alone have adopted as an argument for Slater's guilt as a murderer.

To the credit of some of the jury, the verdict of Guilty was not unanimous. Against nine holding that view, one found Slater Not Guilty and five found the charge Not Proven. Here came in Slater's misfortune at having been tried in Scotland. In England, the division of opinion would have secured him a verdict of Not Guilty and an acquittal. The Scottish system of the majority verdict sealed his fate. He was sentenced to death, adding to the disgrace in which he already stood by so forgetting his manners as to interrupt the passing of sentence with protestations of his innocence. Truly, a vile, despicable foreigner, and a murderer if ever there was one! 'Even if he did not do it, he deserved to be condemned, anyhow', snapped a writer in one Scottish newspaper.

With his execution only two days away, and the scaffold already erected, Slater was reprieved. By no means all Scottish opinion had been jaundiced by the colour of his disreputability. A petition on his behalf had been signed by more than 20,000 people, many of whom, though happy to have seen such a blackguard brought to public trial, could not in conscience accept that the proof of his guilt had been conclusive enough to justify hanging him. The Press supported the demand for a reprieve, and a convincing review of the facts of the case forwarded to the Secretary for Scotland by Slater's lawyers did the trick. His sentence was varied to life imprisonment.

'It is an atrocious story, and as I read it and realized the wickedness of it all, I was moved to do all I could for the man', Conan Doyle wrote. Wrote the famous criminologist, William Roughead, another determined campaigner on Slater's behalf: 'That paladin of lost causes and champion of forlorn hopes … spared neither time nor money nor energy in his conflict with the embattled forces of the Circumlocution Office… He applied to the problems presented by the case the expert methods of Mr. Sherlock Holmes.'

Conan Doyle's booklet *The Case of Oscar Slater* appeared in August 1912, by which time Slater had been in jail for more than three years. As with Edalji, he tore the case against Slater piece by piece to shreds. As with the Edalji case, an alternative suggestion was presented: Holmes again — 'One should always look for a possible alternative and provide against it. It is the first rule of criminal investigation.'

Conan Doyle's alternative was so simple that it had occurred to no one. ('It has long been an axiom of mine that the little things are infinitely the most important.') Why, with expensive jewellery lying all about him, had Miss Gilchrist's assailant contented himself with stealing only a diamond crescent brooch? Even allowing for his having been disturbed, he could have snatched up more than that. And why had he wasted time rifling a box of papers? Conan Doyle's suggestion — and to this day no one has offered a more convincing one — was that a document, not jewellery, had been the intruder's object. He had entered the bedroom, lit the gas, searched hastily through the papers, then, pausing only to snatch up a piece of jewellery to mislead the police, had walked calmly past Helen Lambie and Mr. Adams and taken to his heels.

What kind of a document? A will? The search for a will would imply an intruder with a family connection. This, in turn, would explain how the murderer had gained entry to the locked and barred flat. Miss Gilchrist, whose habit it had been to observe any callers through a window before opening the door to them, must have recognized him and admitted him without fear, resuming her seat beside the fire without the least fear of assault. The theory of a visitor known to her would further explain the apparent calmness of his having lit the gas in the bedroom in order to examine the documents, and — more startling still — the fact that Helen Lambie had expressed no surprise to Mr. Adams at finding a strange man in the flat on her return from her errand. Perhaps it was because the man was no more a stranger to her than he had been to Miss Gilchrist. ('The real murderer is standing immediately behind you!')

Plausible though it was, this Holmesian theory left the authorities unmoved. Slater continued to languish in gaol. Then, after another two years, something occurred which seemed to bear out what Conan Doyle had written.

In 1914, a Glasgow police detective-lieutenant named Trench revealed through a lawyer that on the night of the Gilchrist murder, Helen Lambie had named a man known to her as the person she had recognized leaving the flat. Trench had tried at the time to get his superiors to listen to this piece of evidence, but they had ordered him to ignore it. The matter had remained on his conscience, until, having been concerned in another case remarkably similar to the Gilchrist murder, in which another wholly innocent man had come within an ace of trial and execution, he could keep silent no longer. The lawyer, named Cook, obtained for Trench what he believed to be the security of an authorization from the Secretary for Scotland to reveal what he knew, and Trench made a statement claiming that Helen Lambie had recognized the man in the flat and had admitted as much that same night to a female relative of Miss Gilchrist, a Miss Birrell. ('There was her statement, Watson, and to me, as you can imagine, it was like a light on a dark night.')

Enquiries were made. Both Lambie and Miss Birrell denied that any such remark had been made. But in view of this and other statements made by Trench, there was no alternative but to order an official enquiry. The authorities assuaged their resentment by holding it in secret, with the prisoner not represented. The witnesses were 'invited' to answer questions, but were not placed on oath. Little wonder that the enquiry achieved nothing and that the Secretary of Scotland could feel justified in taking no further action.

Someone was taking action, though — action, once more, of a most disgraceful kind. Trench's superiors suspended him from duty on a trumped-up charge of making information available to another person (the lawyer, Cook) without authority. Trench appealed to the Secretary for Scotland, whose permission he had sought beforehand. There was no reply. After twenty-one years' service, in the course of which he had been awarded the King's Medal for exemplary and meritorious service, he was sacked. Nor did his persecution end there. He and Cook were arrested the following year on another unjustifiable charge. They were acquitted at their trial, amid applause, on the direction of the judge; but they had spent three months in prison awaiting the hearing. Sir Arthur Conan Doyle, however, was not a vulnerable member of the Glasgow police force. With other devoted men, such as the Scottish journalist William Park, and the eminent jurist Sir Herbert Stephen, he continued to press for justice for an unlikable foreigner serving a life sentence for an unsolved crime which he certainly had not committed. Once again, Conan Doyle met the costs himself. His expenditure in terms of time in which he might have been writing profitable stories could be calculated in terms of many thousands of pounds. And he little realized that it would be 1928 — twenty years after the murder of Miss Gilchrist — before the battle for Slater would be won. ('There are one or two details which are not finished off, and it is one of those cases which are worth working out to the very end.')

In *A Study in Scarlet*, Watson refers with wonderment to the number and variety of Holmes's callers at 221B Baker Street. 'One morning a young girl called, fashionably dressed, and stayed for half an hour or more. The same afternoon brought a grey-headed, seedy visitor, looking like a Jewish pedlar, who appeared to me to be much excited, and who was closely followed by a slip-shod, elderly woman. On another occasion an old white-haired gentleman had an interview with my companion; and on another, a railway porter in his velveteen uniform.'

These, as Holmes explains, are his clients — 'people who are in trouble about something, and want a little enlightening'.

Conan Doyle had his unlikely visitors too. One of them, to his Sussex home in 1925, was a convict, just released from Peterhead jail. Adrian Conan Doyle remembers his father showing him the scrap of screwed-up paper which the man had brought him, smuggled out of prison in a hollow tooth. It was a message from Oscar Slater, begging Conan Doyle to make one more effort on his behalf. He had now served fifteen years, the period after which even a genuinely convicted 'lifer' could expect to be released. 'A client is to me a mere unit, a factor in a problem,' says Holmes. 'The emotional qualities are antagonistic to clear reasoning.' It was not on sentimental grounds that Conan Doyle again re-opened the struggle for Slater's release. No passionate plea could aid him so long as the facts supporting his innocence continued to be ignored. Conan Doyle and Sir Herbert Stephen made another attempt to get the Secretary of State for Scotland to reconsider the evidence. There was a long delay, then a refusal.

Two more years passed. Then the case came to the forefront again, with the publication of a book by William Park. Edgar Wallace, whose public was huge for whatever he chose to write, reviewed it at great length. Other newspapers took up the cause and soon found the Slater case to be a circulation-builder over which to compete, vying with one another to unearth any new scrap of evidence. Suddenly the looked-for sensation emerged. An interview was published with Helen Lambie, now married and living in America, in which she was stated to have admitted that the man seen leaving Miss Gilchrist's flat after the murder had been known to her and had often visited the old lady.

The newspaper printing this interview claimed it to be the most dramatic development ever recorded in a criminal case. Unfortunately, Helen Lambie refused to back it up with a testimony under oath. She had told many lies before; but this statement, whether true or false, did the trick. Another newspaper tracked down Mary Barrowman, now a middle-aged married woman, in the hope that she, too, would provide some equally sensational revelation. They were not disappointed. She was prepared to sign a statement to the effect that at Slater's trial she had not wanted to say anything more positive than that he was *like* the man she had seen run away from the murder house; but that the Procurator-Fiscal had ordered her to say that the man had been Slater, and had made her attend his office every day for a fortnight to rehearse the evidence she would give in court.

Conan Doyle and others, sensing that the moment had come at last when their appeals could no longer be ignored, demanded official action. They got it. Like Edalji, Slater was released from prison. There was no mention of a pardon, a public enquiry, or of compensation. He had served nearly nineteen years.

Conan Doyle was not satisfied. He sent a circular letter to Members of Parliament requesting their support in getting for Slater what he had still not had — justice. The Members questioned the Scottish Secretary in the House. The case was officially referred to the new Scottish Court of Criminal Appeal. A public enquiry was ordered.

'It was my fortune to accompany Sir Arthur Conan Doyle daily throughout the proceedings,' writes William Roughead of the hearing in June 1928. 'Next to the appellant himself none of the auditors was more keenly interested in the result.'

The proceedings dragged on, with a break, to late July. It is sufficient to say that Slater's appeal was upheld, by no means unquestionably, but sufficiently for the Court to order his conviction to be quashed. 'It is done now, and we must be thankful for what we have got', Conan Doyle commented. Slater wrote to him, 'Sir Conan Doyle, you breaker of my shackles, you lover of truth for justice's sake, I thank you from the bottom of my heart for the goodness you have shown towards me.' Incredibly enough, the two men had never met until the appeal hearing.

One recalls Inspector Lestrade's words to Jonas Oldacre in *The Norwood Builder.* 'You have done your best to get an innocent man hanged. If it wasn't for this gentleman here, I am not sure that you would not have succeeded.' The identity of

Miss Gilchrist's murderer never emerged, although, shortly before Conan Doyle's death, he confided it to his son, Adrian.

9: MAN OF MANY CAUSES

'It was difficult to refuse any of Sherlock Holmes's requests, for they were always so exceedingly definite, and put forward with such an air of mastery.'

The Edalji and Slater cases are the two major examples of Conan Doyle/Holmes investigations into criminal affairs. The vast Conan Doyle archives contain details of many more that are less known, covering in total a great part of his life after the turn of the century. October 1910 found him taking keen interest in the trial of Dr. Crippen. In March 1925 he was publicly stating his unease over the pathological evidence which had helped to condemn Norman Thorne, the Crowborough chicken farm murderer. The family of a Polish nobleman, suspected of murder, offered to send him a blank cheque if he would come to Warsaw and look into the facts: he had to refuse.

One of his most characteristic investigations, in which he deliberately assumed the thought-processes of Holmes in order to seek the solution, concerned a man who had drawn out his entire bank balance, visited a London music-hall, returned to his hotel, changed out of his evening clothes, and then had disappeared utterly. He had not been seen to leave the hotel, whose doors had been locked for the night not long after his return from the music-hall. The police were baffled and the missing man's relatives approached Conan Doyle by letter. He sent them the correct solution to the mystery by return of post.

The man's having drawn out all his money suggested that his disappearance was deliberate. It could be assumed that he had left the hotel unobserved by mingling with the crowd of returning theatre-goers always to be found in the hall between eleven and eleven-thirty. He would scarcely have left at so late an hour if his intention had been to hide in London: therefore he had gone away by train. A train which would get him to some quiet provincial station at an early morning hour, when he would be noticed and perhaps remembered, could be ruled out. One glance at the timetable reminded Conan Doyle that the expresses to Scotland started from London at about midnight, heading for busy termini where one passenger would never be noticed. He told the man's relatives that they should search in Edinburgh or Glasgow. The former was correct.

But criminal matters were far from being the only ones which called him away from his writing-desk to contribute his enormous energy and influence for the public benefit. As Eden Phillpots said of him: 'Any rank instance of injustice instantly won a swift response from Conan Doyle and, without one selfish thought of fear, he would sanctify his whole great resources to righting what he felt to be wrong or reversing any verdict that he deemed unjust.'

Thus, one is not at all surprised to find him fighting on at least two occasions for the Faith which he himself had seen fit to abandon — Roman Catholicism. He fought for Catholics to be allowed to have a university of their own in Dublin, jeopardizing his chances of election to Parliament by doing so. Later, after the death of Queen Victoria, he wrote to *The Times* protesting against that section of the Coronation Oath which insulted the Roman Catholic faith. Courtesy to all creeds should be the policy of the Crown, was his contention; and a swift end to mediaeval rancours would be a happy beginning for the new reign. His suggestion was adopted.

Yet, within a few years, he was campaigning just as vigorously for a reform to which Catholics as a faith could only be bitterly opposed. He was drawn to the foremost ranks of the Divorce Reform Union by the realization that 'the foundation of national life is not the family. It is the *happy* family. And that, with our obsolete divorce laws, is what we haven't got.' These laws prevented all but the rich from obtaining anything but a judicial separation. A working-class wife could be kicked to death without obtaining her freedom from a drunken, brutal husband. Adultery was still the only recognized matrimonial offence. Conan Doyle was one of those who pressed, with eventual success, for divorce to be made possible in the case of desertion for three years or more, cruelty, incurable insanity or drunkenness, and imprisonment under commuted death sentence.

His concern when it came to his love of justice was not only for his fellow-countrymen. The year 1909 saw the publication of one of his most outspoken works, *The Crime of the Congo*. At first, even he had not believed the reports of slavery and sadism which had been trickling from the Congo for years. When at last he had come to believe he had no hesitation in wielding just as vigorously those weapons with which he had once fought for the British soldier, this time on behalf of the oppressed peoples of a far-off Belgian colony which he had never even visited. Once again, a 60,000-word 'booklet' was the result, every fact and statement it contained checked and counterchecked for accuracy and scrupulously fair interpretation. Once more he would accept not one penny profit. One of the leaders of the agitation in Britain for help for the suffering Congolese wrote later: 'It was not his book — excellent as it was — or his manly eloquence on the platform, nor the influence he wielded in rallying influential men to our cause, which helped us most. It was just the fact that he was — Conan Doyle; and that he was with us. His whole personality appeals to some of the finest and most robust qualities in the English race.'

Not every affair with which he busied himself was quite so momentous. In 1909, in the midst of his Congo campaigning, he accepted only too eagerly the unanimous invitation of several American sporting factions to referee the forthcoming World Heavyweight Championship fight between the great Jim Jefferies and the coloured contender, Jack Johnson. As those who tried to dissuade Conan Doyle were quick to point out, this promised to become more than a trial of boxing skill. Jefferies was white and Johnson coloured, and the result of their meeting could be 'dynamite'. This was not, however, the reason why, after a week's consideration, Conan Doyle refused the invitation. The more urgent and far-reaching Congo question demanded his full attention and must take priority over a matter of mere sport.

Two years later he was again summoned to figure prominently in one of the highest spheres in international sport. As President of Britain's Field Sports Association he was invited at the suggestion of Lord Northcliffe to mediate in the dispute surrounding the financing and training of the British team for the next Olympic Games, a task which was to take up a year of his time.

The year 1912 found him duelling in print with George Bernard Shaw in protest against the latter's jeering scepticism at the reports of heroism of passengers and crew aboard the sinking *Titanic*. In 1913 one of his chief causes was the Channel Tunnel, a project in keeping with his prophetic vision of the value of such a link with the Continent both in peace and war.

The possibility of war in Europe was by now uppermost in his mind. In February 1913 the *Fortnightly Review* published another controversial article by him, *Great Britain and the Next*

War. 'The element of danger is the existence of new forms of naval warfare which have never been tested in the hands of competent men, and which may completely revolutionize the conditions. These new factors are the submarine and the airship.'

The sort of senior officers whom he had offended years before with his strictures on their handling of the South African campaign were still not prepared to take him seriously. His threefold proposal — a Channel Tunnel, a submarine fleet capable of keeping Britain supplied with food without interception, and a self-supporting agricultural economy — was regarded as altogether too absurd. He went a stage further, publishing a long short story, *Danger!*, in which he portrayed vividly a type of warfare in which submarines would hunt merchantmen and be themselves hunted by Q-boats and aircraft. To ensure that his prophecies did not go overlooked in the places for which they were intended, he got his editor to invite the opinions of Naval experts. He might have known the sort of thing to expect. 'I do not myself think that any civilized nation will torpedo unarmed and defenceless merchant ships'; 'I think it most improbable, and more like one of Jules Verne's stories than any other author I know.' These were among the reactions of senior Naval officers.

Only two years later the German Naval Secretary was able to say in the Reichstag: 'The German people can thank the British Admiralty for disregarding the warning on U-boat warfare given by Sir Arthur Conan Doyle.'

The month which preceded the outbreak of war saw the publication of *Danger!* — July 1914. Characteristically, the old campaigner was quick to get into uniform, as Private Sir Arthur Conan Doyle, 4th Volunteer Battalion, Royal Sussex Volunteer Battalion. The idea was his, the organization the forerunner of the Home Guard of the Second World War. Where Crowborough, Sussex, led, communities all over the country followed. In spite of an early attempt by the War Office to crush the self-organized volunteer units out of existence there were eventually some 200,000 men, ineligible to join up, but still capable of carrying a weapon and marching at least ten miles, under part-time training.

Conan Doyle endeavoured to join up for front-line service, in any capacity in which they would have him. His offer was declined. He turned his restless mind once more to the war at sea. He was not as surprised as most other Britons when, with the war only a few weeks old, three old British cruisers were torpedoed by a U-boat and sunk with 1,400 hands. He had known it could happen. Warnings were no further use. All he could do now was to try to find some means of helping those other men who must sooner or later find themselves struggling for survival in the sea. He organized the manufacture of an inflatable 'swimming collar', to be supplied to every man in the Royal Navy. He struggled to get the men provided with safety waistcoats and greater numbers of collapsible boats. The Admiralty took heed. It did not trouble to thank him for his efforts; but he was rewarded enough by the thought that the men for whom he had worked might do so. They did. One Able Seaman wrote to him: 'I know only too well many a poor sailor thanks you, although he didn't know it was you he was blessing.'

Later in the war he tried to help preserve soldiers' lives. French soldiers were issued with steel helmets: why not the British? The War Office took up his suggestion. The knights of old days had profited by their armour; why should not the present-day fighting man have bullet-proof clothing? Winston Churchill agreed heartily, remarking that the bullet-proof man and torpedo-proof ships were two great objectives. Conan Doyle worked hard on a design for shields to be used in action and his own garden resounded with the ring of test shots against sheets of various metals. The shields were never adopted, because of the supposed problem of weight, although he had been told at the Ministry of Munitions: 'Sir Arthur, there is no use your arguing here, for there is no one in the building who does not know that you are right.' He visited the British, Italian and French fighting lines and wrote about what he had seen, bringing to the public at home a new realization of what the war was all about and how it was being fought. He noticed many French veterans wearing badges on their uniforms to denote that they had already suffered wounds, and recommended a similar mark of recognition for British wounded. The suggestion was quickly adopted and the 'wound badge' instituted as the forerunner of the wound stripe.

In the midst of all these preoccupations, 1916 found him once more giving of his time and energy, without thought of reward, for the benefit of an individual on the wrong side of the law. This time he was pleading for one who, like himself, came of Irish parentage and had been knighted for his services to Great Britain. This man was Roger Casement.

It had been Casement who, as British Consul at Boma, in the Belgian Congo, had written the report about the ill-treatment of natives which had sparked off the outcry in which Conan Doyle's voice had been so prominent thirteen years before. Now, Casement was imprisoned in the Tower of London, to stand trial on the sombre charge of High Treason. He had, it was alleged, turned up in Germany after the outbreak of war, moving about freely as a privileged person known to the Germans as a willing traitor to England. He had addressed Irish prisoners, persuading them to exchange captivity for membership of an Irish Brigade which would eventually land in their own country — armed and equipped by the Germans — and would seek to overthrow English rule.

Casement's crime, for which he was sentenced to death, was not one with which so ardent a patriot as Conan Doyle could have the least sympathy, and in petitioning for reprieve he was activated very much by the belief that to hang Casement would be to make him a martyr in the eyes of many and provide the Germans with a valuable propaganda weapon. Nevertheless, he also saw Casement as a man essentially honest to his ideals as an Irishman first and foremost, and he believed him to be mentally afflicted as a result of his long years of service in taxing conditions. The man was unfit to plead and should be sentenced to anything but death. Many eminent men signed the petition; but, rightly or wrongly, Casement was hanged in Pentonville Prison on August 3, 1916.

Casement lost his life. By pleading for him, Conan Doyle, as he later learned, sacrificed the Baronetcy which was to have been his, much as he deliberately gave up the certainty of a Peerage some years after by continuing his support of Spiritualism.

The war took two men very near and dear to himself: his son Kingsley and his brother Brigadier-General Innes Doyle, C.M.G., D.S.O., the little page of Southsea doctoring days. Conan Doyle and Sherlock Holmes, had seen their words come true: 'There's an east wind coming … such a wind as never blew on England yet. It will be cold and bitter, Watson, and a good many of us may wither before its blast.'

In the Napoleonic War three had died of the five members of the family who served. In the Great War, of the seven who went, only one returned. Through the attrition of war, the old line of fighting men was drawing to its close.

10: A CASE OF IDENTITY

'There is only one man'

Of the fourth and last of the long Sherlock Holmes stories, *The Valley of Fear*, which appeared in 1914, Conan Doyle remarked lightly, 'I fancy this is my swan-song in fiction.' It was not, of course. It was followed by most of the stories which comprise the volume *The Case-Book of Sherlock Holmes*, as well as a number of non-Holmes stories. But to all intents and purposes his days as a fiction writer were over. The remaining years until his death in 1930 were to be devoted to what he came to consider to be his greatest crusade of all, passing on the message and comfort of Spiritualism to all who would listen to it, both in his own country and throughout the continents of the world. Thirty years of study lay behind his views upon this controversial subject, and those who would follow him from scepticism to belief can do no better than to read his *History of Spiritualism* and other works such as *The New Revelation* which made up the bulk of his literary output during the post-war years.

But before taking a virtual leave of Holmes he had selected — quite unconsciously — one story in which to plant the clearest of the many clues which identify him with his immortal character. This was *His Last Bow*, published in 1917, and the last, chronologically speaking, of Holmes's adventures.

It is 1914. Holmes is called in, as Conan Doyle had been so many times, to help England. Now it is a world problem that faces him. Graver issues than those of civil crime are in question. To rout the Prussian agent, Von Bork, Holmes chooses the disguise that reveals him to his readers more clearly than ever before. He is an Irish-American motor mechanic: Irish for Conan Doyle's motherland, American for the country to which he had always been so warm a friend. His assumed name is Altamont, the second name of Conan Doyle's father. Holmes and the faithful Watson avert the betrayal of England; but Holmes foresees, as Conan Doyle saw, that by the time the coming war was over the world would have undergone such a change as never before. The prophet, man of action, soldier-patriot at last allowed the detective to stand beside him and claim kinship.

Looking back over Holmes's life, the similarities between him and his creator stand out strikingly. Each came from a line of country squires, with art in the blood. Each had his Watson. Each solved his problems by observation and logical deduction.

Adrian Conan Doyle recalls vividly his youthful walks with his father over the moors of Ashdown Forest, then a fairly desolate expanse of country, 'when his eyes were always on the watch for Stone Age arrowheads and other flints among the heather… I am standing with my father looking down at the wheel marks on a damp moorland track leading from a neighbour's house. "Osmond has been out on his cycle," I said. "I wonder if he's called on us." "Do try to be more observant, my dear lad," reproved my father kindly. "Osmond uses Palmer tyres. These are the marks of Dunlops."'

Both liked working in solitude, in old dressing-gowns; both carried out chemical tests, smoked pipes, carefully compiled scrapbooks on all manner of subjects, but were dreadfully untidy in dealing with papers and personal possessions. Each kept on his desk a magnifying-glass, and in a drawer, a pistol. Both Conan Doyle and Holmes were excellent boxers. They shared the same bankers; they were each offered a knighthood in the same year. Both were brilliant pioneer criminologists, with lessons to teach the detective forces of the world. 'In over a thousand cases I am not aware that I have ever used my powers upon the wrong side,' Holmes could assert. Conan Doyle made no such claim, but his record makes it for him, because, like Holmes, he used those powers on the right side, to save innocent men from prison and the gallows.

In the early days of the Holmes stories the public saw none of the links between their detective idol and his creator, and had no cause to seek them. Holmes, to them, had a vivid reality in his own right. This being so, what would have been easier than for Conan Doyle to have made Holmes his personal mouthpiece, his propaganda vehicle in the crusades which took up so much of his life? Yet, in all the utterances of Holmes (and he made some very profound ones) there is hardly one of which it can be said, 'Ah! There speaks Conan Doyle.' Not a political opinion, or a reflection of the world crises which so occupied Conan Doyle's mind. Not a word of the vulnerability of the soldier and sailor. No plea for the reform of the divorce laws, or for religious freedom. Not one scrap of propaganda for Spiritualism, about which he cared so passionately. If the public's hero, Sherlock Holmes, had spoken up for these things there would certainly have followed a wave of interest and support. Conan Doyle's artistic integrity forbade him.

All the same, one likes to fancy Holmes marching side by side with his creator in his campaigns — under strict anonymity, of course: for, as Watson tells us, 'His cold and proud nature was always averse, however, to anything in the shape of public applause, and he bound me in the most stringent terms to say no further word of himself, his methods, or his successes.'

A NOTE TO THE READER

If you have enjoyed this book enough to leave a review on **Amazon** and **Goodreads**, then we would be truly grateful.

Sapere Books

Sapere Books is an exciting new publisher of brilliant fiction and popular history.

To find out more about our latest releases and our monthly bargain books visit our website:
saperebooks.com

www.ingramcontent.com/pod-product-compliance
Lightning Source LLC
Chambersburg PA
CBHW072047040426
42447CB00012BB/3055